i 2

FOR YOUR GARDEN

Walls, Walks, and Steps

FOR YOUR GARDEN

Walls, Walks, and Steps

GORDON KURTIS

Grove Weidenfeld
New York

A FRIEDMAN GROUP BOOK

Copyright © 1992 by Michael Friedman Publishing Group, Inc.

Published in the United States by
Grove Weidenfeld
A Division of Grove Press, Inc.
841 Broadway
New York, New York 10003-4793

Library of Congress Cataloging-in-Publication Data
Kurtis, Gordon.
    Walls, walks, and steps / by Gordon Kurtis. — 1st ed.
        p. cm.
    Includes bibliographical references.
    ISBN 0-8021-1411-3
    1. Gardens—Design.   2. Garden walks.   3. Walls.   I. Title.
SB473.K87   1991
717—dc20   91-12273
                                                           CIP

WALLS, WALKS, AND STEPS
was prepared and produced by
Michael Friedman Publishing Group, Inc.
15 West 26th Street
New York, New York 10010

Editor: Sharon Kalman
Text Editor: Karen Spinks Stearns
Art Director: Jeff Batzli
Designer: Susan Livingston
Photo Editor: Anne K. Price

Typeset by Bookworks Plus
Color separation by United South Sea Graphic Art Co., Ltd.
Printed and bound in Hong Kong by Leefung-Asco Printers, Ltd.

First Edition 1992
10 9 8 7 6 5 4 3 2 1

Dedication

Dedicated to my Mother and Father,
who always encouraged me to
pursue my own interests.

Acknowledgments

I would like to express my gratitude to the following
people who have made this project possible: Corey
Mundweiler for his belief in my work; Robert Fletcher
for the use of his extensive library of research materials;
and John Greenlee for giving me the opportunity.
I wish to extend a special thanks to Karen Stearns
and Brenda James.

Table of Contents

Introduction

othing is more intriguing than a garden. Nothing makes a greater statement of life and society than architecture. What, then, could be more fascinating than the marriage of the two—that which has been called "garden architecture?"

Since the beginning of time, gardens have evoked feelings of romance and intrigue, whether through the mystery of a deep, dense forest or the intimacy of a courtyard rendezvous. Flowering plants, trees, and shrubs of all kinds have been bringing us pleasure for centuries and have always been part of our lives in one way or another. I have, for years, been fascinated with these garden settings; I am delighted to share with you a topic so dear to my own heart.

Most people have, in a moment of fantasy, envisioned their ideal garden, and those visions tend to be similar—para-

Lush plantings and the interplay of color and texture make the garden a place of beauty and interest.

© Derek Fell

dise. A lush, tranquil retreat. An oasis of unspeakable beauty. A place that inspires the mind and stimulates the senses. An atmosphere in which to think, or perhaps to touch the deeper feelings of the soul.

Gardens are places that allow us to feel the beauty of nature and to reflect upon ourselves; they inspire us to understand our place in this grand creation. And, not only can a garden be a place of incredible beauty, it can be functional as well, creating a barrier to shield us from the outside world's unwanted stimuli; providing one's own personal retreat. A garden can serve a more practical purpose by giving forth a bountiful supply of fruits, nuts, berries, and other delights that are edible, not to mention the visual beauty and fragrance they provide.

Whatever your purpose in creating a garden of your own, the implication is the same: we have always been fascinated with nature's perfect beauty and we will forever strive to make it an integral part of our immediate surroundings. It is here, in creating your own "paradise," that the

aspect of design comes into play. The garden designer's role is an important one. Just as an interior designer develops and defines the home's interior spaces,

Using similar plants to line a walkway accentuates the movement or flow of the path and provides color and fragrance along the way.

Tulips and hyacinths are placed in containers on a low garden wall to add interest and color. Planting in containers is particularly good for gardens where space is limited.

the garden designer develops outdoor "rooms" to further enhance the total outdoor environment. In many instances, if climate permits, the gardens and terraces are mere extensions of the interior spaces of the house, and provide places for entertainment in addition to everyday use and enjoyment.

This book, *Walls, Walks, and Steps,* is dedicated to three of the essential elements that make up "garden architecture," to their uses and to their purpose. Walls help to establish or enclose a given space; walks provide a means of getting from one established space to another; and steps help deal with a change in topography, and indicate a starting or stopping point.

Walls, walks, and steps play a significant role in recreating the beauty found in Nature—and in adapting that created environment to suit our wants and needs: to create a place that more accurately represents our idea of "paradise." By taking into consideration the purpose these elements serve, the materials they are made of, and their proper placement, you can approach the design of your garden in a much more professional way, creating in a more efficient manner and with a more powerful impact, your perfect place.

© Charles Mann

© Charles Mann

Mounds of geraniums line the walkways of this garden.

A hedge window serves as a garden wall, treating garden visitors to a view of what is yet to be explored.

This book is intended to serve as a source of inspiration, to introduce, to explain, and then to illustrate the various settings, presentations, and moods found in gardens throughout the world. It will allow you to explore the endless possibilities of what you can create in your own garden, whether you prefer a quiet place—and a chance to escape with a good book—or a lush setting for cocktails with a few friends. It is possible to create a retreat of your own.

Hiring A Landscape Architect Or Garden Designer

Most garden design or landscape architectural improvements can best be achieved by selecting the proper designer to suit your wants and needs.

Most design work is acquired through referrals, therefore if you know of family or friends who have worked with someone they were pleased with, that is a good place to start.

You will want to choose a person who is accomplished or sensitive to the style that is appropriate to the architectural elements of the project and/or the style you have chosen and would like to achieve on your property.

Ask to see projects previously designed and installed in order for you to formulate an opinion and judge whether you feel the designer is qualified and talented. Meet the designer at the job site where the work is to be done—so that you can walk the property, discuss your wants and needs, any problem areas, what you would like to see developed on the site, and how much money you want to invest. Listening to his or her input, ideas, and concepts will help you ascertain if a working relationship is possible. You must feel comfortable with each other, and the designer should be sensitive to the project and show a genuine interest in it.

If you are working with an architect on the structural elements of your home, he or she can often refer you to a qualified landscape architect or garden designer that they have previously worked with. Again, referrals from others are your best, and safest, bet.

Landscape architects are governed by the State Board of Landscape Architects. A list of landscape architects in your area can be obtained from them.

Low walls that facilitate level changes can be built to blend in with their surroundings.

© Derek Fell

chapter one

Walls

Climbing roses and honeysuckle vie for space on a stone wall. Stone garden walls can easily be covered with foliage and flowers, making them seem less harsh and conspicuous.

© Charles Mann

In creating your garden paradise, you must first create the primary enclosure; that is, the defined garden space. By enclosing your intended garden space, you create a personal sanctuary, an environment ready to be developed as you want it, shielded from the outside world. (Gardens derived their name in Persia, where they were called *pairidaeza*, *pairi* meaning "around" and *daeza* meaning "wall," thus our word paradise.)

There are several factors that influence the location you should choose for your garden. Two of the primary factors to consider are the topography of the land and its views.

How the architecture is situated on the property and its relationship to the street greatly influence the size and type of the enclosure and can be a major factor in determining placement for optimum privacy and security.

One way to establish a primary enclosure is through the introduction of a perimeter wall, either on the property line or as the boundary of the garden. The material you choose for this wall will depend on the feeling you want to evoke, any existing materials on the site (if any), and the style of the garden you wish to create. The most commonly used materials consist of brick, wood, or stone. A chain link fence coated with either green or black plastic, with a combination of espaliers (vines or vinelike plants trained on the fence) and shrubbery can provide security and, eventually, privacy.

Another way to establish an enclosure is by manipulating the contours of the topography, either by removing the soil and lowering a particular area, or by adding low walls and plants. This creates a difference in the relationship of the spaces by changing their elevation and defining the lowered, or step down area as its own element.

Another type of enclosure is the courtyard, which utilizes between one and four

© Charles Mann

existing walls from an adjacent building. History is full of interior courtyards; they were intended as gathering places where residents could interact and socialize, safe and protected, the walls providing a barrier against the unsafe world. Originally, courtyards functioned primarily as a place for ritual washing before prayers. The garden contained only the architecture, water, and its reflection.

In Muslim gardens, the courtyard or enclosed garden fosters order and balance. A traditional pool provides a focal point. The mood is restful and creates a feeling of harmony with nature.

Enclosing the garden space shields it from the outside world and helps it to provide that escape we so desperately seek. And the idealism of the protected environment can be further emphasized by using materials that bear no resemblance to those outside the garden. For example, asphalt is commonly used to pave streets and sidewalks; therefore, it wouldn't be appropriate in a garden. Rather, it would serve as a constant

Vinelike, climbing plants define and soften the architectural elements of this wall and gateway.

A classic example of a hedge row serves as a wall that divides the various parts of the garden into outdoor "rooms."

reminder of the world outside. Gardens provide escape from the overdeveloped world; materials used to create that "safe haven" should be as natural as possible.

The most ideal perimeter walls should be six feet (1.8 m) or higher (if possible), made of soft-colored stones with irregular shapes and deep mortar joints to give the effect of age. Old bricks and rough-cut lumber can also be used to create a proper backdrop for your garden. (Keep in mind that these materials should be compatible with the architectural style of your house and other structures.)

A wall will help to create seclusion and unity. The materials you use to build your walls will help to establish the character of your paradise: brick, wood, or stone each lends an entirely different personality to the space it defines.

Stone is a natural complement to plants. It is also suitable for hillsides, becoming part of the surroundings without detracting from the natural beauty. Using materials that are sensitive to surroundings creates a more relaxing mood. The eye more readily accepts what it sees, without distraction or confusion.

If height restrictions are a limitation for enclosing your garden, remember that walls or fences can be combined with plant material for extra height.

Privacy in a residential area is often limited to six feet (1.8 m), but ivy trained to grow on top of a fence or a wall can provide an additional two feet (60 cm) or more, which may be just what you need to achieve total privacy.

Planter walls, anywhere from 2 to 4 inches in height and up to 4 feet or more, either freestanding or combined with taller walls, minimize the impact of the taller wall. They can also function as seatwalls if their height is within sixteen to eighteen inches (40 to 46 cm), providing seating to garden viewers. For example, by building an eighteen-inch (46 cm) high raised-bed planter wall immediately adjacent to a six-foot (1.8 m) perimeter wall, the visual impact is reduced by a foot-and-a-half (46 cm)—so that the eye sees a four-foot-six-inch (1.4 m) high wall. If plants are part of the raised bed, the impact of the six-foot (1.8 m) wall is reduced even further.

This secluded retreat is created by a profusion of conifers and evergreens. Stone seats are built right onto the stone wall, providing a restful spot.

© Charles Mann

With the primary enclosure established, the perimeter of the garden area has been defined. Now it's time to organize that space.

Look at it; walk through it. Do you feel comfortable there? Is it too large? Do you feel lost? Is it private enough to provide escape? Depending on the size and feel of the defined area, you may want to change the appearance of it, to make it look larger, to cover an obtrusive view, or to break it into smaller compartments (rooms).

If your garden feels too small, remember that illusions can be created through the use and placement of certain materials. Consider using old materials, such as used brick salvaged from demolished old buildings. Combinations of sizes of brick may be used, and flagstone or cobble gives an interesting look. Even broken concrete is an option. In small courtyard spaces, these tend to distract attention from how small the space really is, by drawing attention to the richness of the material.

In large expanses, the flow of strong lines is desirable because it gives a feeling of visual movement and emphasizes the space.

If the intended space feels too large, your paradise may seem too impersonal. Dividing and organizing the space gives perspective, a greater feeling of control, and more comfort. (It can also make the space more useful.)

The climbing rose 'Blaze' spills over a stone wall to add a splash of color. The roses and the evergreen help to integrate the wall into its surroundings.

© Anita Sabarese

Secondary Enclosures

One way to reduce the feel of the overall garden is through the use of internal walls or secondary enclosures. These divide the garden into exterior rooms that can then be further developed to suit your particular needs.

There are three types of secondary enclosures: fences, screens, and internal (lower) walls.

fences

Fences are a very common enclosure that help define spaces in a garden. A fence may separate the pool area from the main terrace, the vegetable garden from the display garden, or the main expanse of lawn from the potting bench.

Fences used correctly on sloping land can greatly affect climatic factors, especially if frost is a consideration in your area. Placement of a solid wall up slope from your property protects from frost flowing downhill, and conversely an open fence placed on the downhill slope allows cold air to flow.

Fences can be made of wood or wire, can be plain or fancy, can act as a barrier, or can simply suggest a boundary. They can be open (like lattice work) to capture breezes, or closed (like a stucco wall) to block wind or reduce noise.

© Charles Mann

Hollyhocks soften an adobe wall. A low wall can define an exterior space and still allow the visitor to view the surroundings.

This garden wall, composed of brick columns softened by white climbing roses with lattice wooden panels, provides the feeling of privacy while still allowing a view.

Screens

A screen can be a combination of plant material and structural enclosures, such as a louvered wooden panel with an espalier (vine) attached to it.

A screen can also be a privet hedge pruned to the desired height and clipped neatly to maintain privacy. The hedge provides privacy from the street level. Combine it with a row of small trees to block the view of a neighbor's house overlooking your garden.

Screens, like fences, can help protect the garden by diminishing the wind, but usually are more decorative. They also can provide privacy by covering unsightly utility areas or by controlling the movement (traffic flow) of guests. Oftentimes the spot with the best view can be windy. A wind screen, usually made of a solid see-through material such as clear acrylic panels or glass, can protect viewers from harsh winds and leave the view unobstructed. (Be aware that wind screens also intensify heat in the immediate area.)

Screens also can be used to conceal seasonal gardens that are out-of-season, or areas reserved for cut flowers or vegetable gardens that may not look attractive year round. Some screens can even be removable, a true advantage for the times when certain areas are blooming.

© Derek Fell

Other internal walls

An example of an internal wall made of something other than a screen of wood or lattice is called a "swag." Swags are a combination of wooden posts that provide support and rope or chain used as the lateral or horizontal connections between the posts that have some type of climber (a flowering vine) growing on them.

Many variations of swags can be created to obtain the desired effect. It may be a low decorative element, such as a picket fence; or perhaps a tall screen between garden spaces. Because of their graceful line, swags fit nicely into gardens that contain curves.

In choosing your walls, screens, or fences, remember that, in garden architecture, "form follows function." What it will look like—or what it will be—depends on what it should do. Once you've decided what you want to accomplish, how to accomplish it becomes an easier decision to make.

Let's consider the hierarchy of enclosures: perimeter walls will be the tallest (six to eight feet—1.8 to 2.4 m—or more), followed by internal walls whose heights vary according to use (such as screens). All of these elements combine with plants to establish the garden structure.

© Charles Mann

To create a garden that truly appeals to the sense of romance, boundaries introduced by walls, plants, and combinations of the two should not all be seen from one vantage point. More than one vantage point allows for interest and intrigue, stimulating a sense of adventure and curiosity. Maintain your element of surprise and you create a sense of discovery.

© Derek Fell

Opposite page: *Climbing plants embellish an arching framework and lure the eye to the garden beyond.* Left: *Combining plants with hardscape elements, such as this stone wall, unifies all of the elements.*

Self-clinging vines can quickly cover a garden wall and, if left to grow naturally, will dramatically soften its impact.

Vines, Climbers, And Wall Plants

Since walls can usually be found quite readily in any garden setting, whether they are part of the house or another structure or introduced for the purpose of mere pleasure, they can be integrated into the garden by softening and accentuating them with plant material. And there are many ways to do this.

Self-clinging vines can be used effectively on a wall and, if left unchecked, will soon cover it completely. They have a capacity to soften and reduce the impact the structural surfaces have on the garden. Vines such as *Parthenocissus tricuspidata*, most commonly referred to as Virginia creeper or Boston ivy, are fast growing and adaptable to a wide variety of climates. There are many varieties and cultivars available, most of which have a five-pointed maplelike leaf that is a bright, shiny green color throughout spring and summer. During the fall, the leaves respond to the change in temperature by turning a bronzy, coppery color accentuated with shades of yellow and red. The vine is deciduous, meaning that it will lose its leaves in the winter. (This varies according to region and climate.) In temperate climates the loss of leaves in the fall is slow to come, and in early spring it leafs out quickly. In some instances, it may not lose its leaves entirely during the deciduous season.

Ivies can provide a leafy background to highlight other plants in the foreground of the garden. They are hardy, rigorous, and dependable, occasionally performing all too well. The large-leaved *Hedera canariensis*, or Algerian ivy, can quickly fill in a chain link fence to provide privacy and a lush backdrop for a garden setting. If introduced onto architectural elements or structures, Algerian ivy can be invasive, if not properly maintained. Smaller-leafed varieties such as *Hedera helix* 'Hahnii' or the variegated leaves of *H. h.* 'Goldenheart' introduce a much finer texture and are more versatile. Ivies can also be used most effectively as ground covers underneath larger shrub plants or used in planting beds. If left to roam naturally, they can have a softening effect and introduce a more casual atmosphere.

The plants that bloom with intoxicating fragrances or have interesting and unusual leaf structure tend to provide a more romantic atmosphere than do the ivies: vines such as *Passiflora caerulea*, the passion vine, with its lavender, star-shaped flowers that are reminiscent of water lilies; or *Campsis radicans*, the trumpet creeper, with its long orange and scarlet flowers, can easily draw attention or high-light an area in any garden with their spectacular displays of color.

How vines are incorporated into the garden depends upon the effect you want. Most climbers and vinelike plants tend to be thought of as loose and informal, but many have the capacity to be very well-groomed and can be trained in a variety of different ways. The method by which a plant is trained on a wall by some means of support is called espalier.

To espalier a plant against a wall, the main branches are attached to the surface either by trellis work, wire, or a similar means to fan or train the growth over the surface. Working the branches in a formal

California Glory (Fremontodendron californicum) *is espaliered on a brick wall with its main branches running parallel to the mortar joints, leaving the beauty of the brick to show through.*

© Charles Mann

© Charles Mann

The coppery foliage of the dwarf Japanese maple (Acer palmatum) *adds contrast to the surrounding green foliage.*

or patterned method will produce a design or accentuate a wall and provide an attractive means for the plant to grow.

Many shrubs and evergreen trees can be trained on a wall or fence using the espalier method. Species like *Magnolia grandi-flora*, the southern magnolia, with its large, glossy green leaves and large white flowers with citruslike fragrance, make a beautiful cover. There are many varieties of *Camellia japonica* to choose from and all afford a clean, dense coverage with any

© Nancy Hill

array of flower sizes, colors, and styles. *Camellia virginiana* is a good choice for gardens located in colder climates. Check your local sources for other shrub and tree suggestions.

Another method of softening and accentuating walls with plant material is through the introduction of "spills." Climbers or vinelike plants atop walls in containers and in strategic locations let the flowers and foliage tumble down the face of the surface. This can be a very effective look when there is an area of the garden that is in need of softening, but which may not have the space to accommodate planting. This method will also draw the eye upward, creating the illusion of more space than there actually is.

Walls can be constructed with a planter at the top so that plants can be planted directly into the wall. Planting pockets can also be made part of the vertical surface of the walls, allowing for alpines, phlox, helianthemum, campanula, and similar material to fill in spaces by sprouting from nooks and crannies on its face.

Walls can be constructed of peat blocks, which easily develop beautiful mosses and lichens. Although this method of construction is limited to a maximum height of eighteen inches (46 cm), it creates a very unusual effect.

Walls can be made of sod itself. This method was used by the ancient Romans in areas where other building materials were scarce. In Hadrian's Wall in northern Britain, entire sections were made of grass sod. Sod can be cut into pieces one foot (30 cm) in width and eighteen inches (46 cm) in length, then stacked, sloping inward, and inverted as they are laid.

A similar method can be used to stack broken concrete pieces for low walls. This creates plenty of spaces for plant materi-

Planters built into garden walls can add color and interest where space is limited.

als to integrate into the space and become a part of the wall itself, creating a very naturalistic approach to retaining soil in a sloping area.

Plants can serve as walls themselves. Many varieties of junipers, arborvitae, and hollies can make a very effective boundary. *Cupressocyprarus leylandii*, Leyland cypress, as well as *Buxus*, boxwood, and *Taxus*, yew, can establish a dense "wall" of plant material, providing all the privacy you need with a lovely soft green background.

Candytuft (Iberis) *and alyssum* (Aurinia) *have been planted at the base and on top of this stone wall. A dry stack or mortarless stone wall can provide cracks and crevices for plants to pop through, giving the wall a more natural look.*

© Derek Fell

Combining plants is an effective "wall" also; *Polygonum baldschuanicum*, the bokhara fleece-flower, when used with tall grasses can be practical and attractive.

Climbing plants, in combination with fences and screens, can be an exciting element in the garden, in addition to being functional.

© Charles Mann

Plants that provide good cover with little support are *Clematis armandii*, the evergreen clematis, and *Rhynchospermum jasminoides*, star jasmine. Both have glossy green leaves and fragrant flowers. Other hybrids of *Clematis* (some requiring less pruning) are 'Duchess of Edinburgh,' 'W. E. Gladstone,' and 'Lasurstern.' *Pyracantha*

is hardy, tolerant of many climates, and has many varieties. Most have strong branching structures that are very striking on a wall. All have beautiful displays of berries that hang on the vine for long periods of time, and also attract birds.

Spectacular bloomers can also be found in *Wisteria sinensis* 'Alba,' with its grapelike clusters of white flowers festooned from its twining branches. Planting it on a garden structure such as an arbor lets the blossoms hang from above, making a striking display. *Hydrangea petiolaris*, the climbing hydrangea, with its lacy flowers, sprinkles open-faced clusters wherever it is allowed to sprawl. It blooms in the fall, when most of the garden is "at rest," making it a welcome addition.

Color and interest can not only be brought into the garden by flowers, but also by fruit-bearing vines. Ornamental grapes with dark colored fruits and pubescent leaves make attractive displays on walls and fences. Varieties such as *Vitis vinifera* 'Brant,' 'Apiifolia,' 'Incana,' and 'Purpurea' are just a few.

Left: *An iron railing on a stone terrace makes an attractive support for this rambling grapevine.*

chapter two

Walks

When you introduce a walkway into a garden you are orchestrating and conducting the movement of the user. The primary purpose of a walk is to provide a logical, organized transition from one established space to another. Of course, that's the stated purpose, but, actually sometimes half the fun is getting there.

A path not only leads to a garden experience, but can actually be the experience in itself: passing by carefully tended beds of flowering shrubs and blossoms, slicing through an expanse of lawn, or tiptoeing through a shady side yard filled with annuals and perennials. Have you ever experienced a walk caressing the edge of a cliff to capture a view?

Catnip billows over the crushed stone walkway as if standing guard; it also serves to guide garden visitors to the upper terrace.

© Charles Mann

There may be many tempting distractions along the journey—including the intrigue of what lies ahead—for the walk dictates movement and controls it throughout the garden. Walks not only connect spaces, they also organize how we view the garden, emphasizing site lines and directing one's attention. In a garden, a walkway can lead to many elements: a fountain, a statue, a bench.

Paths and walks are the underlying structure of the garden. Plan carefully before you begin incorporating them into any garden setting.

In planning a garden, you should take into consideration the functional needs of the walkway, the visual effect or impact that it will create in your garden, the theme or style you wish to maintain, the amount of traffic the walkway must accommodate, and its environmental constraints (such as topography).

Be sensitive to the architectural elements that are already part of your garden and proportion the walkways to them. This will make it easier to make your

© Charles Mann

walks appear an integral part of their surroundings.

In designing walkways—like walls—form depends on function. A good garden design is merely an answer to a question or problem.

Typically, a walk should be at least four feet (1.2 m) in width to accommodate two people walking comfortably side by side. City sidewalks in suburban areas are usu-

An archway frames the view, while a stone bench doubles as sculpture. Roses bordering the lawn path accentuate this focal point.

This grass walkway is a perfect compliment to the informal nature of the garden.

© Charles Mann

ally five feet (1.5 m) wide. The size relates back to the user, its purpose, and what part of the garden it serves.

From a practical standpoint, you should try to create walkways that will reflect safety, efficiency, and a pleasing sensitivity to the user. From an aesthetic point of view, your goals should be to excite the senses and the spirit, and to exclude reason in favor of emotion through thought-provoking materials.

A visitor embarks on two journeys when experiencing a garden. One is actual, the other is imagined. The walk serves as a vehicle to explore the actual surroundings, but the true measure of a successful garden is when all of the elements come together, in order for the mind to wander.

Gardens are constantly referred to as the symbol for paradise. The beauty of the garden to the Muslim is held to be a reflection of God. And God has actually described paradise as a garden. No wonder we try to create our own, here on earth.

Gardens are considered the soul, or spiritual side, of the relationship of a building to its landscape. If the building is analogous to the body, then the garden is its spirit.

By controlling the size of your spaces and their relationships to one another, by balancing intimacy with openness and shade with sun, you create a stimulating sensation that makes the experience even more memorable.

The basic concept of paths today has its roots in religion. Ancient civilizations, whose lives were dominated by their religious beliefs, created elaborate gardens and temples to honor the living and the dead. In Egypt, one of the most dramatic examples of a walk is found at the mortuary temple of Queen Hatshepsut at Deir-el-Bahari, built around 1500 B.C. The long, linear approach from the gated entry evokes an emphasis of "onward and upward." The processional "path" is a series of terraces and walkways that direct the visitor on a central axis to the uppermost level of the structure.

At this temple, spaces were equally divided so that gardens could be viewed from both sides, but more importantly was the belief that when the eye looks at two points it immediately "sees" a third one, virtually the exact center between them. Thus, the flow of movement was dictated to form a procession down the center, or midpoint, between the two "sides." This approach was quite prevalent throughout Egyptian development.

The Walk's Function

The functional aspect of a walkway is to provide a sensible surface from which to view the garden, and to heighten the experience by bringing the visitor closer to the elements that make up the various spaces. Being able to traverse the area at a flowing, comfortable pace, the walk provides a means of experiencing the garden

© Derek Fell

A stone path and bridge guide the visitor through the Ryoanji Temple garden in Japan.

from different vantage points, making it possible not only to view the garden from afar, but actually to immerse yourself in the garden and experience it firsthand. Paths and walkways can also serve as part of the overall design on the ground plane (horizontal surface) by creating patterns and shapes that, when viewed from above (such as a second-story window or roof deck), can be interesting in itself. Many formal gardens were designed with that very intention. The purpose of the walk also dictates its layout. The formal and the informal approaches provide two main organizational concepts. The formal layout is usually symmetrical or on a strong axis with mirrored images. An informal garden has a more natural feeling to it, with curvilinear shapes that are more free flowing. These shapes can often be determined by the garden's natural surroundings, existing architectural elements, or a combination of the two.

In utilizing a formal layout, a simple, functional garden design amplifies a sense of order. The grid pattern for walks and paths used in Monet's gardens at Giverny are very formal and linear, yet when the garden is in full bloom the plants spill over their borders, softening the straight lines and formality.

Oriental gardens typically evoke a passive feeling with an emphasis on viewing and strolling. The layout is usually more curvilinear and fluid. Although the structure can be formal because of the careful attention to the placement of plants and other elements found in the garden, the feeling is one of harmony. Paving is one of the most important features found in ori-

A classic rose garden with boxwood hedge and crushed rock walkways is laid out in the rectangular fashion reminiscent of English gardens.

© Charles Mann

ental gardens. Natural paving materials, including pea gravel, crushed rock or stone, flagstone, and slate, that are sensitive to their surroundings and that articulate rhythm and movement are often made part of the design. Familiar oriental gardens, such as the raked sand garden in the Monastery of Ryoanji, in Japan, and the gardens of the Forbidden City in Beijing are classic examples of paving patterns evoking movement and rhythm. Once you've decided the walk's purpose, the next step is to determine the types of materials the walk will be constructed of.

Nasturtiums sprawl profusely over the Grand Allee of Monet's garden, adding an informal and romantic quality.

Right: *Combinations of materials, such as brick and stone, create interesting patterns on the ground plane.* Far right: *Stone laid in a checkered pattern adds texture and visual appeal.*

Choosing The Materials

In choosing the materials for your walks, try to maintain a sense of unity with the other elements in the garden, especially those that require paving. Try to keep a continuity throughout your driveways, entrances, patio spaces, or the paving around garden structures to reinforce the theme of the garden design.

The color of the material, its texture, and scale can vary, greatly affecting the mood that your walk creates. Take the time to explore these materials. The garden experience is full of exploration and discovery, and the walk is the method of getting there.

Walks that are used frequently or for transporting items from one space to another on a regular basis would be more practical if the material were comprised of a hard surface, similar to or repeating those used for walls: brick, stone, flagstone, concrete, and slate are all suitable choices for a more permanent walk.

Remember that these walks are linking house and garden, in addition to providing a lure into the garden. Both are of utmost importance.

Materials such as pebbles or aggregate added to concrete can introduce an interesting texture and color while providing a non-slick surface to walk on. Rugged and irregular surfaces evoke a slower pace, as

Far left: Patterns of textured concrete can either be left in their natural state or colored. Left: "Pockets" of plantings interspersed throughout paving materials add interest and relief.

does a narrower path. Squared or rounded cobbles can be very effective in adding texture. Smooth materials, such as flagstone laid with mortar, provide a more practical surface in areas where snow removal is a consideration. When using stone, it is usually best to choose whatever is native to your region. Native stone usually will appear more natural, and can be less expensive, since you avoid the cost of importing.

Allow for the encroachment of plantings from nearby beds—a common mistake is making the path too narrow. This not only limits the walkway's ability to accommodate more than one person at a time, but also makes it uninviting.

Stone, a wonderful, natural material, can be set in sand or with a concrete base and mortar. Stone set in sand can have grass or ground-cover joints (the space between the stones) in lieu of mortar. With the introduction of plants (creeping herbs, perennials, and ground covers), the stones take on a whole different feeling. "Crazy paving" is the technique of laying irregularly shaped pieces of large stone at random, creating a pattern of interlocking shapes.

Tiles also make a suitable surface. Thick, handmade tiles can be very attractive, giving the garden walk a sense of history and romance. These are more suited to milder climates.

© Charles Mann

Concrete, although sadly overlooked, can be versatile and manipulated in many ways by the introduction of color and texture. In addition to being practical and cost effective, it is a logical choice for many garden settings. Practical, inexpensive, and pleasing to the eye, precast concrete pavers can be purchased in many sizes and shapes and in a variety of material combinations. Combined with a low-growing ground cover between them, they can make an attractive path through any garden space.

Bricks come in many shapes and sizes and can be laid in many patterns. The most recognizable patterns are herringbone, basketweave, and running bond. Much of Gertrude Jekyll's work with architect Sir Edwin Lutyen during the nineteenth century involved laying brick on its long narrow side to create a whole new look and feel, evoking an entirely different character—all just by using a common material in a different way.

Brick can be set in sand, usually more appropriate for areas of light traffic, or with concrete base and mortar for a more stable surface. Although the latter is more expensive to install, the surface is more durable. Climatic regions with expansive soils or areas with large surface roots from trees can cause bricks on sand to shift and lift in places. Make sure the site is suitable for the type of installation you choose.

Wood decks and boardwalks are excellent where the setting requires an elevated surface, either near waterways or over rough terrain. Remember that wood needs periodic upkeep and can be slippery when wet.

Informal or casual paths can be made up of softer materials such as rock chips, grits, bark chips, lumber, cobbles, and coarse sands in combination with step pads of concrete and stone.

Pine needles, licorice root, shredded pine bark, or wood chips would all be appropriate in a woodland setting.

Some loose materials may require an edging to keep them in place. Metal strips, redwood headerboard, landscape ties, or rocks work well if containment and a defined edge are called for. Even plants with a low, ground-hugging character can contain loose paving materials. Certain varieties of liriope, if planted directly at the edge of the path or walk, have a capacity to keep loose material under control. Because of their nature, the looser, more rugged materials require periodic replenishing.

Grit is a naturally occurring phenomenon underneath large trees in woodland settings. Over long periods of time large raindrops fall from the foliage to the ground underneath the trees, causing the larger particles to rise to the surface.

Opposite page: *Repetition of materials can enhance or exaggerate a perspective.*
Below: *Softer materials, such as wood and loose stone, can create a casual path to accommodate a change in levels.*

© Derek Fell

A French parterre garden often utilizes crushed rock as a walking surface.

These particles make an excellent natural surface to create a walk or path. The edge can blend gracefully and fluidly into the planting beds or can be kept contained, whichever you prefer. Grit and gravel used around clipped boxwood hedges help to complete what is called the "par-terre" garden, accentuating the outline of the hedge and providing a clean surface to walk on. The garden at Versailles contains classic examples of the "parterre" garden.

Of course, the most simple paths or walkways are those made of packed earth, but climate and terrain can be lim-

© Charles Mann

© Derek Fell

iting factors. Grass paths—cut through taller meadow grass and fields of wildflowers—can work well when getting from one area of the garden to another. Of course, this type of walkway tends to appear more natural. There are two materials suitable as functional and decorative alternatives to lawn: *Holcus mollis* 'Variegatus,' which has a gray-green color accented with cream foliage, and spreads quickly; and *Sisyrinchium angustifolium*, called blue-eyed grass for its vivid blue flowers found in early summer. Both create an informal surface to walk on and combine the natural setting with a practical path.

Although the materials and combinations can be endless, try to avoid letting the walk become too busy and distracting from the overall harmony of the garden design. Remember that it is essentially a functional element.

An important factor to consider when planning a walk is the overall cost of construction and maintenance. Softer materials are relatively inexpensive to install, but can have a high maintenance expense. The more variable materials, such as cobbles or flagstone, are moderately expensive both to install and maintain. The hard-surface materials, such as concrete and brick, can be initially expensive to install but have minimum maintenance requirements.

A mortarless brick path set on sand evokes a loose, informal feel and allows moss and grasses to grow between the crevices.

© Derek Fell

Right: This strip of lawn serves as a pathway, allowing visitors a closer view of the vibrant colors of the rhododendrons and azaleas. Opposite page: *Using scented ground covers between paving stones provides a delightful surprise to those who walk on it. It also helps to conceal the riser face and surrounds its edge, giving it a floating quality.*

"Puddling" is a common problem and a condition easily avoided. All walks should be pitched for drainage and the degree of that pitch varies, depending on the material used. Usually one-eighth inch (3 mm) of a cross-slope for every one foot (30 cm) of width will work well. Earth-packed paths or loose materials should be installed in such a way to allow moisture to fall to both sides and be carried away by channels.

Ground Covers

Ground covers can be effectively combined with pieces of stepping stone by leaving planting "pockets" or strips between the pieces—usually ranging between two to four inches (5 to 10 cm) in width—and incorporating various plants such as mosses or lawn into this area.

These not only add visual appeal to the garden, but by incorporating materials that have a scent to them when crushed under foot, add the delightful dimension of fragrance. Herbs such as creeping thyme or lemon-scented thyme exude a fresh, lively fragrance when trod upon. Chamomile also lends itself well to cracks and crevices between paving, providing a nice contrast to the hard surface.

Peppermint or spearmint not only provide fragrance in the garden, but an occasional pinch or two for an iced tea or a mint julep surely wouldn't be missed. Pennyroyal has uniquely round leaves with a strong mint fragrance, ideally suited for use in and around walks. Most

mints are very hardy and fill in rapidly, providing a lush carpet. Since mints grow by underground stems they have a tendency to be quite invasive if not maintained, so unless you want a more casual look to your garden, you may consider planting them where they can be maintained or you could end up supplying the whole neighborhood with fresh mint.

Many of the fragrant plantings are also intensified by heat, whether a rise in the temperature or reflective heat from a walkway or a garden wall. Make sure you are aware of their surroundings or the fragrance may become overpowering.

Other ground covers that perform well in shade are English ivy and Hahn's ivy. Both work well because their leaves are small. Japanese spurge is an excellent ground cover tolerant of deep shade, but it prefers at least partial sun. It is not as invasive as other ground covers and its rich, dark green leaves with white flower spikes brighten any shady corner.

For planting in milder climates, mondo grass has a most interesting texture. Its

© Balthazar Korab

dark green leaves are almost bladelike, and grow in grassy clumps. It can tolerate full sun in some areas, but looks best in partial shade.

Ground covers can not only provide additional texture, color, and fragrance, but aid in stopping soil erosion and, once established, keep weeding down to a minimum by covering what would be bare soil. (Never one to rest, Mother Nature tends to keep a profusion of unwanted plants appearing in one's garden, brought in by the wind or birds. Even seeds that may be dormant in the ground will fill any opening that is available.)

To accentuate a gravel path and keep the loose stones in place, line it with the plantain lily. Its low, broad leaves guide the eye and reinforce the shape or hard line of the walkway.

A delicate ground cover of lily-of-the-valley adds a touch of fragrance from its small, white, bell-shaped flowers and a once all-too-shady part of the garden suddenly becomes as intriguing as the places bathed in sunshine.

Ground covers are another means of providing color and scent in the garden.

chapter three

Steps

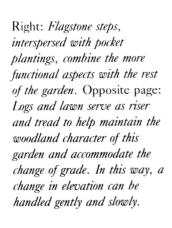

teps can be, and usually are, an integral part of any garden. Their primary purpose is to enable us to go from one topographic level to another comfortably and with ease, in a more practical and aesthetically pleasing manner, when a ramp or slope would be impractical.

From a design perspective, the use of steps in the garden implies movement from one place to another. The placement of the steps, along with their design and the materials used to construct them, determine how much and what kind of movement they will provide.

The materials used to build steps should be determined by the architectural style of your house and other structures on the property. You will want to keep a sense of cohesiveness among existing structures, and choose materials for steps that will add movement and beauty to the

Right: *Flagstone steps, interspersed with pocket plantings, combine the more functional aspects with the rest of the garden.* Opposite page: *Logs and lawn serve as riser and tread to help maintain the woodland character of this garden and accommodate the change of grade. In this way, a change in elevation can be handled gently and slowly.*

© Derek Fell

garden, while still serving their purpose. Steps draw people into a space, but let them feel that they wandered in on their own. Therefore, you don't want to use materials that draw attention to themselves at the expense of the beauty or form of the steps. Use materials that blend with the surroundings, complement the design, and add grace to the garden without becoming obtrusive.

Steps indicate a starting or stopping point, providing a sense of place. They are typically equated with leaving or entering a new space, and they can make a lasting impression. Proper placement, choice of materials, and usable design can make your steps a truly outstanding part of your garden.

Step Construction

There are two basic parts to steps: the tread is the flat surface on which we walk; and the riser is the face or vertical plane between.

© Derek Fell

While maintaining the dominance of the lawn, cut stone laid flush with the lawn guides visitors to steps leading to the upper garden.

Ease of use is important and is dictated by the tread/riser relationship. Purely utilitarian steps, such as those descending into a basement, follow a standard architectural relationship of six-inch-high (15-cm-high) steps (riser height), with a tread (the flat surface you walk on) being at least twelve to fourteen inches (30 to 36 cm) wide. Most steps used in the home fall within or near this ratio.

For outdoor steps, typically, two times the riser plus the tread should equal twenty-six inches (66 cm).

The size and ratio choices for steps are endless, but should stay within the boundaries of usability. The height for a riser should be between four and seven inches (10 and 18 cm). The tread should be maintained at eleven to fourteen inches (28 to 36 cm). Keep in mind, too, that just as the tread and riser must be in proportion, a one-quarter-inch (6 mm) pitch should be included for drainage, allowing rainfall and moisture to run off the tread.

Of course, in gardens, this ratio can and often does vary for the sake of design and aesthetics. For example, with a rise of four inches (10 cm), to create a gentle progression, use the formula: ($2 \times R + T = 26$). So, figure $2 \times 4 + T = 26$ inches; the tread should be eighteen inches (46 cm).

By varying the riser/tread ratio, the pace of the steps' "movement" can be quickened or slowed. Make sure you take into consideration this rule of thumb when planning steps for your garden: narrower flights of steps will tend to separate spaces, making them more individual, while wider steps tend to bring the two spaces together, even making the two appear as one large space.

Low riser height and a wide tread can quicken the pace and make the user appear to be gliding down the steps. This is very useful in situations where the transitions from one level to another should happen easily and gracefully. This type of step would be appropriate where two large expanses of lawn have a change in level; you would want the two "elements" to flow together.

Conversely, steps with a high riser and a narrow tread tend to slow the movement of the user, which can actually be advantageous in a steep slope where one's attention to the slope and its surroundings must be accentuated.

Straight flights of steps tend to be "faster" than those that curve. Long or wide steps are "faster" as well.

In designing your steps, consider their proportion in relation to their surroundings and the purpose they serve.

Think of the step design as it relates to the proportions of the human body. Pets and wild animals can adapt, but steps are made for people; they must not only be in scale and proportion to the architecture and their surroundings, but be comfortable to the human user as well.

© Derek Fell

Decorative tile used on the riser face is an effective way to add color and interest to a flight of steps. The top and bottom of the steps are logical "pause points."

Here are some tips to help you decide when and how to add steps, where to add them, and how many to have.

• Add steps wherever there is a slope or a change in topography that make traversing on a ramped surface impractical. The idea is to fuse the spaces or parts of the garden so that people can go from one space to another. Keep in mind that steps are conducting movement, as well as creating a sense of place. The tops and bottoms of a flight of steps are natural pause points. You have arrived!

• The steps will inevitably lead to a path; your path materials may be similar or contrasting, depending on your intention. Their location is determined by their relationship to the various spaces in your garden and what activities are taking place in those spaces (active or passive), as well as their relationship to each other.

• Depending on the change in ground level that you must traverse, steps should not occur in the landscape more than six at a time. Landings should be provided so the user can pause; this makes the experience more enjoyable and less taxing.

• Two people can walk comfortably side by side if the steps are at least five feet (1.5 m) in width.

• Large expanses of steps can serve a dual purpose by not only providing a way to get from one change of level to another, but also as retaining elements in lieu of a wall, thus maintaining an openness between the two spaces.

• Long, broad steps can also provide informal seating for family gatherings or just the right spot to display some of your favorite container plants. And they create a feeling of luxury and restfulness.

Steps and ramps create an interesting and functional combination that is especially effective when space is limited. The textured concrete ramps function as a driveway up the hill for vehicles, and the stone step inserts serve as a stairway for pedestrians.

© Derek Fell

© Charles Mann

• A small, winding path of steps making its way up a gentle slope can be very intriguing, luring its visitor deeper into the setting. Curve your pathways to the right, whenever possible. The psychological implication of "what's around the corner" usually leads to the right.

• Many gardens don't have a topography that warrants the use of steps. In some instances, changes in elevation are created by contouring the topography to add interest to an otherwise level garden.

Materials

Materials used will greatly impact the look of the steps. Brick, wood, and stone provide an architectural complement and help to determine the garden's character.

Stone steps are particularly appropriate in a woodland setting and provide a more natural feel.

Make sure you take the existing architectural elements into consideration. As with walls, the type of material and the amount it is used throughout the property greatly influence and dictate the strength of character of the steps. Whenever possible, the steps should be integrated into the landscape to become a part of their surroundings and to avoid dominating the charm of a garden setting. Remember to keep in mind the ideal dimensions, the site itself, and the reason for the steps in a garden. This will help you to determine the type of steps most appropriate.

Fletcher Steele, one of the most prominent and original landscape architects of the first half of the twentieth century, says

Pedestals incorporated into a flight of steps display container plants. Terrace, steps, and walkway made of the same material provide a unified look.

Below: *Walls and steps made of flagstone provide an appropriate prelude to the exquisite gardens found on the upper levels.* Right: *A flagstone path winds its way through the ferns.* Opposite page: *Ivy trained on a riser face of brick, along with lawn as an oversized tread, provide a means for people to walk from one level to another.*

of steps, "Garden steps should be plastic . . . . It is pushing and pulling; hollowing and lumping; patting and shaping 'til something emerges which has length, breadth and thickness . . . and a hint of *more*. A hint of movement, of grace promised, of beauty that hides or lies forgotten. It is the curve of the back of a leopard made clear in the rail of a stair."

© Derek Fell

Vines

Just as ground covers can be combined with the stones of a walk, vines, particularly those that are self-clinging, have a wonderful effect when combined with steps. By growing a vine on the vertical face of a set of steps, the integration of paving with landscape is achieved, allowing the steps to meld into the garden—the Virginia creeper does this beautifully. Its self-clinging nature enables it to adhere to the face of a flight of steps, making them disappear and leaving the horizontal surface walked upon seem to float in a mist of greenery. This adds a lush look and a sense of unity throughout the garden.

© Courtesy of Robert M. Fletcher & Associates

Many of the smaller-leafed ivies can be utilized in the same way. It requires a bit of maintenance to ensure that the growth from plants is kept sheered away from the tread or surface to be walked upon. (You don't want to dissuade people from using the steps nor do you want to make the steps difficult to climb.)

Another alternative is to have the tread (horizontal surface) made up of lawn or meadow grass and the riser (vertical surface) made from a landscape material such as a railroad tie, lumber pieces, stone, or brick. The effect is quite interesting and is useful where the change in grade can be made gradually and over a long expanse in a garden. This would not be suitable for slopes or changes in grade that are too extreme, however.

For a sunny spot, add a softening effect with the delicately sweet fragrance of alyssum 'sweet white' with white masses of ground-hugging flower clusters. Add nasturtium with its billowing growth and unusual round leaves to create masses of fragrant orange to yellow flowers.

© Derek Fell

chapter four

Plant Suggestions

The two most important factors to consider in selecting the plants you will use within and between your walls, walks, and steps are the climate in which the various plant materials will be growing, and the function or purpose they will serve in the garden.

Establishing your soil type and climate will help you to better select the types of plants that will grow well in your garden and will give you the healthy, natural look that you want.

Determine Your Climate

In choosing plants, the first thing you must determine is your climatic region. For most plants, the critical factor is the temperature range in your particular part of the world.

Referring to hardiness zone ratings could be a good start. The map on page 92 shows the average annual minimum temperatures in ten geographic zones and lists the approximate minimum tempera-

Right: *Wildflowers thrive in the dappled shade of a thicket of trees. Large canopies of tree cover can make climatic conditions differ from those in the immediate surroundings.*

© Derek Fell

© Lynn Karlin

Most plants are categorized according to their tolerance to or preference for sun and shade. Proper placement of plants is the key to a successful garden. Placement is not only important for the plants' growing requirements, but for the relationship the plants in the garden have to each other. The color, texture, size, reflective qualities, and leaf type all should be taken into consideration. The colors and textures of the plant material can reflect a mood and should complement or contrast with one another, depending upon the feeling you want to create.

Plants can create a sense of order, emphasize a progression of spaces, soften harsh elements, provide privacy, add color and fragrance, accentuate focal points, and evoke a range of feelings. Plants are a lot like people, having their own special and unique character. The combination of dramatic and delicate foliage adds variety and intrigue to a garden. The introduction of plants is another step in transforming your garden to be a reflection of realms of another world.

Left: *Light and heat can reflect off walls and effect the types of plants suitable for the planter area.*

ture a plant will tolerate in winter. These temperatures may vary according to your specific climatic conditions, but they can be helpful in selecting the proper plants. You can also refer to your local botanical garden nursery for information regarding specific plants and their performance in your area. A soil analysis is also very important to help determine your soil type. This will dictate the plants you are able to grow, and tell you how to amend your soil.

Color and texture can provide interest at all levels of a garden, even on a vertical face. Soil and moisture between a stone wall provide the growing medium; you provide the imagination.

Climbers And Wall Plants

Actinidia arguta. **Gooseberry vine. Z4**

- 4 feet (1.2 m) or larger.

- Plant in well-drained soil in sun.

- Clusters of cup-shaped cream flowers in late summer. Oval, prominently veined, dark green leaves.

- Both male and female plants are necessary to produce edible fruit.

Aristolochia durior. **Dutchman's-pipe. Z4**

- 4 feet (1.2 m) or larger.

- Plant in well-drained soil in sun or half-shade.

- Pitcher-shaped yellow-green and brown flowers in midsummer. Large, bold, heart-shaped, bright green leaves.

Key To Charts:

First line: Botanical Name. Common Name. Hardiness Zone

Second line: Height

Third line: Specifications

Fourth line: Description

Fifth line: Notes (if applicable)

© Charles Mann

Campsis radicans. **Trumpet creeper. Z4**

- 4 feet (1.2 m) or larger.

- Plant in well-drained soil in sun.

- Trumpet-shaped orange and scarlet flowers in summer. Pinnate green leaves have up to eleven toothed leaflets.

- *C. r.* 'Flava' has yellow flowers.

- *C. r.* 'Madame Galen' has salmon-red flowers.

Clematis alpina. **Clematis. Z5**

- 18 inches (46 cm) or less.

- Plant in well-drained soil in any situation.

- Nodding blue flowers with white stamens in early summer. Dissected dark green leaves.

- Good on north-facing wall.

Clematis armandii. **Clematis. Z7**

- 4 feet (1.2 m) or larger.

- Plant in well-drained soil in sun or half-shade.

- Clusters of waxy white flowers, with sweet scent, in spring. Oval, shiny, dark green leaves.

Clematis montana 'Grandiflora.' **Clematis. Z6**

- 4 feet (1.2 m) or larger.

- Plant in well-drained soil in any situation.

- Lightly scented white flowers with yellow stamens in late spring.

Clematis 'The Countess of Lovelace.' **Clematis. Z6**

- 24 to 48 inches (60 to 120 cm).

- Plant in well-drained soil in any situation.

- Double, rosette-shaped, blue-violet flowers from summer to early autumn. Finely cut green foliage.

Clematis *species (Clematis).*

Lonicera japonica
(Honeysuckle).

Coronilla glauca. **Crown Vetch. Z8**

• 18 inches (46 cm) or less.

• Plant in well-drained soil in sun or half-shade.

• Clusters of lightly scented, pea-shaped, cream-yellow flowers in spring and sporadically later on. Heavily divided, shiny, light green leaves composed of many, small, oval leaflets.

Hydrangea anomala ssp petiolaris. **Climbing hydrangea. Z5**

• 4 feet (1.2 m) or larger.

• Plant in well-drained acidic soil in sun or half-shade.

• Large, flat-topped, green-white racemes with marginal white florets in early summer. Oval, pointed, bright green leaves.

• Clings with its aerial rootlets.

Jasminum officinale. **White jasmine. Z7**

• 4 feet (1.2 m) or larger.

• Plant in well-drained soil in sun or half-shade.

• Highly fragrant clusters of small, trumpet-shaped, white flowers from late spring to autumn. Pinnate, dark green leaves of five to nine small, lanceolate leaflets.

Lonicera x *americana.* **Honeysuckle. Z5**

• 4 feet (1.2 m) or larger.

• Plant in well-drained soil in any situation.

• Fragrant clusters of white flowers, turning deep yellow, in early summer. Broadly elliptical bright green leaves.

• Purple tinted buds; excellent climbing through trees and hedges as well as on walls.

Lonicera japonica 'Halliana.' Hall's honeysuckle. **Z4**

- 4 feet (1.2 m) or larger.
- Plant in well-drained soil in sun or half-shade.
- Highly fragrant clusters of white flowers, turning yellow, in late spring. Oval bright green leaves.
- Can be invasive in some areas.

Parthenocissus henryana. **Silvervein creeper. Z6**

- 24 to 48 inches (60 to 120 cm).
- Plant in well-drained soil in any situation.
- Three- or five-lobed, dark, velvet-green leaves, with pink and silver veins, turning bright red in autumn.

© Charles Mann

Parthenocissus quinquefolia. **Virginia creeper. Z4**

- 4 feet (1.2 m).
- Plant in well-drained soil in sun or half-shade.
- Five, oval, stalked, green leaflets, with shiny undersides, turning orange to scarlet in autumn.
- Self-clinging, small, blue-black fruit.

Parthenocissus quinquefolia *(Virginia creeper).*

***Passiflora caerulea.* Passion Vine. Z9**

- 24 to 48 inches (60 cm to 1.2 m).

- Plant in well-drained soil in sun.

- Highly scented, star-shaped, white and purple flowers with conspicuous centers in summer and early autumn. Palmate five- to seven-lobed dark green leaves.

- After a hot summer will produce oval, orange, edible fruits.

***Polygonum aubertii.* Silverlace. Z4**

- 4 feet (1.2 m).

- Plant in well-drained soil in sun or half-shade.

- Thick panicles of cream flowers faintly tinted pink from high summer to autumn. Medium to large pale green leaves.

- Quick growing, tolerates poor conditions.

***Trachelospermum jasminoides.* Star jasmine. Z9**

- 4 feet (1.2 m).

- Plant in well-drained soil in sun or half-shade.

- Very sweet-scented, tiny, trumpet, star-shaped, white flowers in late summer. Long, oval, very shiny dark green leaves.

Wisteria sinensis *(Wisteria).*

Vitis vinifera 'Brant.' Grape. **Z6**

- 4 feet (1.2 m) or larger.

- Plant in well-drained soil in sun or half-shade.

- Small, light green flowers in summer. Large three- to five-lobed green leaves turning crimson, orange, and pink in autumn.

- Edible sweet purple-black grapes in autumn.

Wisteria sinensis. Wisteria. **Z5**

- 4 feet (1.2 m) or larger.

- Plant in well-drained soil in sun.

- Long racemes of fragrant, pea-shaped mauve or deep violet flowers in spring. Light green leaves with up to thirteen elliptical leaflets.

- *W. s.* 'Alba' has white flowers and is powerfully scented.

Ground Covers

Achillea ageratum. Yarrow. **Z5**

- 12 inches (30 cm).

- Plant in well-drained soil in sun.

- Large heads of white florets in summer. Filigree-leaved stems.

Armeria 'Bees Ruby.' Sea pink. **Z3**

- 18 inches (45 cm).

- Plant in well-drained soil in sun.

- Deep pink flowers in summer. Glossy green leaves.

Briza minor. Rattlesnake grass.

- 18 inches (45 cm).

- Plant in well-drained soil in sun or half-shade.

- Shimmering panicles of flowers in summer. Long, narrow, grassy leaves. Graceful pendant seed heads.

Campanula barbata var *alba.* Bellflower. Z4

- 1 foot (30 cm).
- Plant in well-drained soil in sun.
- Small, bell-shaped, pure white flowers in summer. Small, straplike green leaves.

Campanula medium 'Bells of Holland.' Canterbury bell.

- 15 inches (38 cm).
- Plant in well-drained soil in sun.
- Large, bell-shaped, blue, mauve, rose, or white flowers in early summer. Small, straplike, green leaves.
- Biennial. Other varieties available.

Ceanothus griseus horizontalis. Carmel creeper. Z8

- 18 inches (46 cm) or less.
- Plant in well-drained soil in sun or half-shade.
- Large panicles of light blue flowers in spring.

Chamaemelum nobile. Chamomile. Z6

- 1 inch (2.5 cm).
- Plant in well-drained soil in sun.
- Tiny, green, slender leaves. Small, yellow buttonlike flowers occur in summer.

Convallaria majalis. Lily of the valley. Z3

- 9 inches (23 cm).
- Plant in well-drained soil in half shade.
- Sweet-scented racemes of bell-shaped flowers in spring. Long, oval, green leaves.
- Good ground cover in shade.

Epimedium grandiflorum. Bishop's hat. Z5

- 9 inches (22 cm).
- Plant in well-drained soil in shade.
- Loose sprays of small, white, bright yellow, deep red, and bright violet flowers in early spring. Shiny green leaves, tinged bronze in autumn.
- Good ground cover, tolerant of dry soil.

Festuca ovina var. glauca. **Blue fescue. Z4**

- 6 to 8 inches (15 to 20 cm).

- Plant in well-drained soil in sun or half-shade.

- Purple flowers in panicles in late spring and summer. Long, thin, silver-blue foliage in dense tufts.

- Tolerant of dry soil.

Hedera canariensis. **Algerian ivy. Z8**

- 4 feet (1.2 m) or larger.

- Plant in dry well-drained soil in shade or half-shade.

- Small green umbels in late summer. Broad five- to seven-lobed light mat green leaves.

Hedera colchica. **Persian ivy. Z7**

- 4 feet (1.2 m) or larger.

- Plant in well-drained soil in shade or half-shade.

- Small green umbels in summer. Very large, ovate, thick, leathery dark green leaves.

Hedera helix. **English ivy. Z6**

- 4 feet (1.2m) or larger.

- Plant in well-drained soil in shade or half-shade.

- Small green umbels in autumn. Three- or five-lobed, dark green leaves.

- Black fruit, also makes excellent ground cover. *H. h.* 'Baltica' hardier (Z5).

Hosta fortunei var. aurea. **Plantain lily. Z3**

- 2 to 3 feet (60 to 90 cm).

- Plant in well-drained soil in shade.

- Mauve florets on each stem in summer. Broad pointed green leaves with variegated golden edges.

Festuca ovina glauca *(Blue fescue grass)*.

Nepeta *x* faassenii *(Catmint)*.

© Charles Mann

Mentha pulegium. Pennyroyal. Z5

- 4 to 12 inches (10 to 30 cm).

- Plant in well-drained soil in sun.

- Small lilac flowers in late summer and autumn. Scented, oval, dark green leaves.

- *Mentha piperita* (peppermint) and *Mentha spicata* (spearmint) are also good varieties of mint to plant.

Nepeta x *faassenii*. Catmint. Z4

- 1 foot (30 cm).

- Plant in well-drained soil in sun.

- Spikes of lavender-blue flowers in spring and summer. Fragrant, small, gray leaves form spreading clumps.

Cats love this plant!

Ophiopogon japonicus. **Mondo grass. Z9**

- 8 to 12 inches (20 to 30 cm).

- Plant in well-drained soil in sun or half-shade.

- Forms dense clumps that spread by underground stems. Dark green leaves with summer-blooming light lilac flowers on short spikes.

Saxifraga '**Cloth of gold.**' **Saxifrage. Z5**

- 3 to 6 inches (8 to 15 cm).

- Plant in cool, moist, well-drained soil in half-shade.

- White flowers in early summer. Golden foliage.

Scabiosa graminifolia. **Pincushion. Z4**

- 10 to 12 inches (25 to 30 cm).

- Plant in well-drained soil in sun.

- Mauve-blue flowers with yellow centers in summer and early autumn. Grasslike silver leaves.

Sedum cauticola. **Stonecrop. Z4**

- 4 inches (10 cm).

- Plant in well-drained soil in sun or half-shade.

- Sprays of small, crimson florets in late summer. Blue-gray leaves in spreading tufts.

Stachys lanata. **Lamb's ears. Z4**

- 20 inches (50 cm).

- Plant in well-drained soil in sun or half-shade.

- Pink flowers in summer. Silvery, soft, felted leaves with low-spreading habit.

Thymus serphyllum var. *coccineus.* **Creeping thyme. Z6**

- 2 to 4 inches (5 to 10 cm).

- Plant in well-drained soil in sun or half-shade.

- Clusters of small red flowers in early summer. Fragrant, threadlike leaves forming creeping mats.

Stachys lanata *(Lamb's ears)*.

Climbing roses, trained around the front door of this house, accentuate the entryway.

Tradescantia virginiana 'Osprey.' Wandering Jew. Z4

- 12 to 18 inches (30 to 45 cm).

- Plant in well-drained soil in sun.

- Three-petaled, white, multiple florets in summer. Straplike, untidy green leaves.

- Sprawling habit.

Vinca minor 'Bowles variety.' Dwarf periwinkle. Z5

- 6 to 9 inches (15 to 22 cm).

- Plant in well-drained soil in shade or half-shade.

- Funnel-shaped, bright blue flowers in spring and summer. Small, ovate, shiny, dark green leaves with trailing, spreading habit.

- Excellent ground cover. Other varieties available.

© Nancy Hill

Climbing Roses

Rosa 'Golden Showers.' Z5

- 8 feet (2.4 m).

- Plant in moist well-drained soil in sun.

- Slightly fragrant, bright yellow flowers, 5 inches (13 cm) across, bloom in late spring and summer. Oval, smooth, glossy, dark green leaves.

- Good on pillars and walls.

Rosa 'Madame Hardy.' Z4

- 6 feet (1.8 m); erect.

- Plant in moist, well-drained soil in sun or half-shade.

- Strongly scented, double, camellia-like, pure white flowers with greenish center in summer. Oval green foliage.

Rosa moyesii 'Geranium.' Moyes Rose. Z6

- 10 feet (3 m); erect, arching.

- Plant in moist, well-drained soil in sun or half-shade.

- Single scarlet flowers, 2 inches (5 cm) wide, with gold stamens in summer. Typical shrub rose foliage.

- Crimson bottle-shaped hips in autumn.

Rosa primula. Primrose rose. Z7

- 6 feet (1.8 m); erect.

- Plant in moist, well-drained soil in sun or half-shade.

- Fragrant, single, flat, pale yellow flowers in late spring. Small, lightly aromatic leaves with seven to thirteen green leaflets.

Rosa rubrifolia. Redleaf rose. Z2

- 6 feet (1.8 m); loose, arching.

- Plant in well-drained soil in any situation.

- Small, single, pink flowers in summer. Oval plum-gray foliage.

- Quick growing. Excellent for hedging.

Climbing roses add to the charm of this white picket fence.

Rosa rugosa 'Parfum de L'Hay.' Rugosa rose. Z4

- 6 feet (1.8 m); bushy.

- Plant in moist, well-drained soil in sun or half-shade.

- Extremely fragrant, double, medium-sized, crimson flowers summer. Oval green leaves.

- Possibly the strongest perfumed rose of all.

Rosa rugosa 'Pink Grootendorst.' Rugosa rose. Z4

- 3 feet (90 cm); erect.

- Plant in well-drained soil in sun or half-shade.

- Large clusters of small, loose, double, pink flowers in summer. Small, wrinkled, green leaves on very prickly stems.

Rosa rugosa 'Blanc Double de Coubert.' Rugosa rose. Z2

- 6 feet (1.8 m); arching.

- Plant in well-drained soil in sun or half-shade.

- Strongly fragrant, large, semidouble, pure white flowers in late summer. Small green leaves.

Perennials

Acanthus mollis. Bear's breech. Z5

- 3 feet (90 cm).

- Plant in dry, well-drained soil in sun or half-shade.

- Purple or white flowers on tall spikes in summer. Rich, glossy green leaves.

© Charles Mann

Aconitum carmichaelii. Monkshood. Z4

- 4 feet (1.2 m).

- Plant in well-drained soil in half-shade.

- Pale, hooded, rich blue flowers in late summer and autumn. Dissected green foliage.

- Provides good late-season color.

Agapanthus patens. Lily-of-the-Nile. Z7

- 2 to 3 feet (60 to 90 cm).

- Plant in well-drained soil in sun.

- Clear blue flowers cluster at top of stem from midsummer to early autumn. Straplike green foliage.

- Lightly mulch crown in winter.

Anemone japonica 'Kreimhilde.' Japanese anemone. Z5

- 30 to 36 inches (76 to 90 cm).

- Plant in well-drained soil in sun or half-shade.

- Erect, clear pink flowers from late summer to autumn. Divided green foliage.

Aconitum carmichaelii
(Monkshood).

Aquilegia biedermeier. Columbine. Z4

- 18 inches (45 cm).

- Plant in well-drained soil in sun.

- Erect stems of pink flowers in summer. Dissected light green foliage.

- *A.* 'McKana' has flowers of mixed colors.

Artemesia absinthum. Common wormwood. Z5

- 36 inches (90 cm).

- Plant in well-drained soil in sun.

- Fragrant panicles of little, tight, yellow globes in summer. Fragrant, finely dissected silver-green leaves.

- Herb used to make absinthe.

Aster sedifolius. Aster. Z6

- 3 feet (90 cm).

- Plant in well-drained soil in sun or half-shade.

- Daisylike light blue to mauve flowers in late summer. Small, narrow, green foliage forming clumps.

Astilbe 'Ostrich plume.' Meadow Sweet. Z4

- 2 to 3 feet (60 to 90 cm).

- Plant in moist soil in half-shade.

- Pendant, bright pink flower spokes in early summer. Finely divided green leaves forming clumps.

- Good for massing.

Bergenia cordifolia. Heartleaf bergenia. Z6

- 15 inches (38 cm).

- Plant in well-drained soil in any situation.

- Clusters of drooping lavender-pink flowers on each flower spike in late spring. Large, oval, shiny, green leaves in untidy clumps.

- Quick growing, needs shade in winter.

Catanache caerulea. Cupid's dart. Z4

- 2 feet (60 cm).

- Plant in well-drained soil in sun.

- Semidouble blue flowers in summer. Long, straplike hairy leaves.

Centaurea montana. **Dusty miller. Z8**

• 15 inches (38 cm).

• Plant in well-drained soil in sun.

• Pink, violet, or purple flowers in early to midsummer. Oblong, arching, silver-gray leaves in clumps.

Cheiranthus **'Bowles mauve.' Wallflower. Z6**

• 3 feet (90 cm).

• Plant in dry, well-drained soil in sun.

• Racemes of mauve-purple flowers in spring and intermittently throughout year. Narrow gray leaves.

Cimicifuga racemosa. **Snakeroot. Z3**

• 4 feet (1.2 m).

• Plant in moist, well-drained soil in shade. Slightly fragrant, long, tapering, feathery, white plumes in mid- to late summer. Small, deeply cut, toothed green leaves.

Delphinium x *belladonna* **'Blue bees.' Delphinium. Z3**

• 38 inches (97 cm).

• Plant in moist, well-drained soil in sun.

• Tall, packed, open, cap-shaped, sky-blue flowers on single flower spike in early to midsummer. Deeply dissected green leaves in clumps.

• *D.* × *b.* 'Lamartine' has violet-blue flowers, 48 to 84 inches (1.2 to 2.1 m).

Centaurea montana *(Dusty miller).*

***Dicentra exima.* Fringed bleeding heart. Z3**

- 18 inches (45 cm).

- Plant in well-drained soil in half-shade.

- Sprays of locket-shaped, pendant, pale-rose or white flowers in spring and summer. Fernlike green leaves in mounds.

Dicentra *(Bleeding heart)*.

© Charles Mann

***Echinops ritro.* Thistle. Z3**

- 4 to 6 feet (1.2 to 1.8 m).

- Plant in well-drained soil in sun.

- Round-shaped, steel-blue flowers in summer. Divided, spiny, blue-gray leaves.

***Euphorbia alpinum.* Spurge. Z6**

- 4 feet (1.2 m).

- Plant in dry, well-drained soil in sun or half-shade.

- Clusters of yellow-green flowers in early summer. Gray-green foliage.

***Geranium pratense.* Cranesbill. Z4**

- 2 feet (60 cm).

- Plant in well-drained soil in sun.

- Single, soft, lavender-blue flowers in summer. Leaves form bushy shape.

- *G. p.* var. *alba* has white flowers.

Gypsophila paniculata. **Baby's breath. Z3**

- 3 feet (90 cm).

- Plant in well-drained soil in sun.

- Loose delicate sprays of small, single, white blooms making fluffy clouds in summer.

Hemerocallis 'Happy returns.' **Daylily. Z4**

- 18 to 36 inches (45 to 90 cm).

- Plant in well-drained soil in sun or half-shade.

- Trumpet-shaped lemon-yellow flowers in summer. Straplike green leaves forming mounds.

Heucherella tiarelloides 'Bridget bloom.' **Coral bells. Z3**

- 10 to 12 inches (25 to 30 cm).

- Plant in well-drained soil in half-shade.

- Sprays of small, white to pink bell-shaped florets in late spring to midsummer and again in early autumn. Small, slightly lobed leaves in compact domes.

Iberis sempervirens 'Snowflake.' **Evergreen candytuft. Z4**

- 18 to 24 inches (45 to 60 cm).

- Plant in well-drained soil in sun or half-shade.

- Pure white florets forming rounded flower heads in late spring and early summer. Small dark green leaves.

- Light shade in winter.

Gypsophila paniculata *(Baby's breath)*.

Kniphofia erecta *(Red-hot poker)*.

Iris kaempferi. Iris. **Z5**

- 30 to 36 inches (76 to 90 cm).

- Plant in moist, well-drained soil in sun.

- Large, open, snow-white, blue, or purple flowers in early summer. Erect, thin, striplike green leaves in clumps.

- Many different cultivars available.

Kniphofia erecta. Red-hot poker. **Z8**

- 4 feet (1.2 m).

- Plant in dry, well-drained soil in sun.

- Poker heads of packed, orange-scarlet florets on erect, flowering stems in late summer. Swordlike green leaves form untidy clumps.

Liatris pycnostachya. Gayfeather. **Z3**

- 4 feet (1.2 m).

- Plant in well-drained soil in sun.

- Fluffy, rose-purple flower spikes in midsummer. Thin, arching, green foliage.

Oenothera missouriensis. Evening primrose. **Z4**

- 12 to 18 inches (30 to 45 cm).

- Plant in well-drained soil in sun.

- Funnel-shaped yellow flowers that open at evening in summer. Small, oval, green leaves forming mounds.

Paeonia lactiflora. Paeonia. **Z3**

- 2 feet (60 cm).

- Plant in moist, well-drained soil in sun or half-shade.

- Strongly scented, large white flowers in early summer. Large, dark green leaves.

- Many different cultivars available.

Papaver orientale 'Goliath.' Oriental poppy. **Z3**

- 3 feet (90 cm).

- Plant in well-drained soil in sun.

- Single, open, bright red flowers in late spring and early summer. Long, fernlike, hairy, green leaves in clumps.

- Pink and white cultivars available.

Pennisetum alopecuroides. Fountain grass. **Z6**

- 1 to 5 feet (30 to 150 cm).

- Plant in well-drained soil in sun.

- Flowers in summer. Long, thin, green, yellow, or purple leaves in clumps.

- *Pennisetum setaceum* var. 'Cupreum' has reddish leaves.

Phlox douglasii. Phlox. **Z4**

- 4 inches (10 cm).

- Plant in well-drained soil in sun.

- Lavender-pink to white flowers in spring. Dense, dark green foliage.

- Both deciduous and semievergreen.

Polygonatum commutatum. Solomon's seal. **Z3**

- 30 inches (76 cm).

- Plant in moist, well-drained soil in shade.

- Multiple, drooping, white flowers flushed with green on arching stems in spring. Elongated, oval, green leaves.

© Derek Fell

Primula auricula. English primrose. **Z5**

- 6 to 10 inches (15 to 25 cm).

- Plant in moist, well-drained soil in any situation.

- Clusters of narrow, bell-shaped, green flowers with circle of cream toward center in late spring before leaves appear. Large, waxy, light green leaves.

- *P. a.* 'Lovebird' has light green petals.

Primula veris. Cowslip. **Z5**

- 9 inches (22 cm).

- Plant in well-drained soil in sun or half-shade.

- Clusters of drooping, lemon-yellow florets in spring. Light green leaves forming rosettes.

Papaver orientale *(Oriental poppy).*

***Primula vulgaris.* Primrose. Z5**

- 4 to 8 inches (10 to 20 cm).

- Plant in moist, well-drained soil in shade or half-shade.

- Single, open, buttercup-yellow flowers with golden centers in spring. Puckered, light green leaves in rosettes.

***Ranunculus graminicus.* Ranunculus. Z6**

- 15 inches (38 cm).

- Plant in well-drained soil in sun.

- Cup-shaped yellow flowers in late spring and early summer. Narrow, grasslike leaves in small clumps.

***Salvia x superba.* Sage. Z4**

- 3 to 4 feet (90 to 120 cm).

- Plant in well-drained soil in sun.

- Multifloret, violet-purple flower spikes in summer. Fragrant gray-green leaves.

- Drought and heat tolerant.

***Solidago canadensis* 'Golden thumb.' Goldenrod. Z3**

- 1 foot (30 cm).

- Plant in well-drained soil in sun.

- Feathery panicles of deep yellow florets in early summer. Elongated, golden-green leaves.

***Viola odorata* 'Queen Charlotte.' Sweet violet. Z6**

- 3 inches (8 cm).

- Plant in well-drained soil in sun or half-shade.

- Fragrant, small, open, deep blue flowers in spring. Small, oval, green leaves in small clumps.

Salvia x superba *(Purple sage)*, *foreground*.

© Wolfgang Kaehler

Annuals & Biennials

Annuals and biennials can be planted in all zones once the danger of frost has passed.

Alcea rosea var. *nigra.* Hollyhock.

- 5 feet (1.5 m).

- Plant in well-drained soil in sun.

- Chocolate-maroon flowers, black toward center, in summer. Rough-toothed, heart-shaped, light green leaves. Can be grown as an annual or biennial.

Alyssum 'Sweet white.' Alyssum.

- 3 inches (8 cm).

- Plant in well-drained soil in sun or half-shade.

- Fragrant, small, white flowers from early summer to early autumn. Short, straplike leaves form spreading mounds.

© Charles Mann

Alcea rosea *(Hollyhock).*

Antirrhinum 'Lavender monarch.' Snapdragon.

- 14 to 16 inches (35 to 40 cm).

- Plant in well-drained soil in sun or half-shade.

- Mauve-pink multiflowered spikes from early summer until frost. Small, dark-green leaves on flower stem.

- Dead-head for repeat blooming.

A cutting garden with annuals. Marigolds, zinnias, and snapdragons make delightful cut flower arrangements.

© Derek Fell

Cineraria maritima. Cineraria

- 6 to 8 inches (15 to 20 cm).

- Plant in well-drained soil in half-shade.

- Neat, fernlike, woolly, silver-gray foliage.

- Can be grown as annual or biennial.

Dianthus caryophyllus. Carnation.

- 18 to 36 inches (45 to 90 cm).

- Plant in dry well-drained soil in sun.

- Pink carnation flowers, strongly clove scented, in summer. Narrow, waxy, gray leaves in clumps.

- Biennial or short-lived perennial.

Digitalis purpurea. Foxglove.

- 5 feet (1.5 m).

- Plant in well-drained soil in sun or half-shade.

- Massed in hanging, bell-shaped, bright pink flowers, with mottled insides, on long erect spikes in summer. Oval, soft, gray-green leaves.

- Biennial *D. p.* var *alba* has pure white flowers; 4 feet (1.2 m).

- *D. p.* 'Apricot' has apricot flowers.

Impatiens 'Futura wild rose.' Balsam.

- Plant in well-drained soil in shade or half-shade.

- Small, iridescent, cerise flowers throughout summer. Small, oval leaves.

- Quick growing. *I.* 'Futura white' has single white flowers. *I.* 'Saper elfin white' has bright white flowers.

- Var. 'Wallerana' grows well in milder climates.

I. purpurea. **Morning glory.**

- 200 inches (5 m).

- Plant in well-drained soil in sun or half-shade.

- Flowers in shades of white, pink, blue, and mauve in summer. Triangular green foliage.

- Quick-growing flowers open only in the morning.

Lathyrus odoratus 'Aerospace.' **Sweet pea.**

- 6 feet (1.8 m).

- Plant in well-drained soil in sun.

- Fragrant, large, white flowers in summer. Oval, light green leaves.

- Quick-growing climber.

  L. var. 'Marietta' has rose-mauve flowers.

Lobelia 'Blue basket.' **Cardinal flower.**

- 4 to 6 inches (10 to 15 cm).

- Plant in well-drained soil in sun or half-shade.

- Violet-blue flowers with white eyes throughout summer. Small, narrow, lance-shaped, toothed, green leaves.

- Half-hardy.

Matthiola bicornis. **Stock.**

- 12 inches (30 cm).

- Plant in well-drained soil in sun. Spicy, fragrant, single lilac flowers in summer. Long, thin, midgreen leaves.

- Biennial.

Myosotis sylvatica. **Forget-me-not.**

- 12 inches (30 cm).

- Plant in moist, well-drained soil in half-shade.

- Small, rich, blue flowers in early summer. Small, lance-shaped, green leaves in compact mounds.

- Annual or biennial.

Nigella damascena 'Miss Jekyll.' Love-in-a-mist.

- 18 inches (45 cm).

- Plant in well-drained soil in sun.

- Semidouble cornflower-blue flowers in summer. Delicate, finely cut, green foliage in feather clumps.

Papaver 'Fairy wings.' Poppy.

- 10 to 14 inches (25 to 35 cm).

- Plant in well-drained soil in sun.

- Single flower heads of mixed pastel shades of pink, white, and gray-blue in summer. Small, furry, light green leaves in clumps.

- Frequently self-seeds.

Papaver rhoeas. Poppy.

- 2 feet (60 cm).

- Plant in well-drained soil in sun.

- Single, bowl-shaped, scarlet flowers with golden stamens all summer. Green leaves in clumps.

Petunia 'Snowcloud.' Petunia.

- 9 to 12 inches (22 to 30 cm).

- Plant in well-drained soil in sun or half-shade.

- Soft, petaled, pure white flowers all summer. Small, oval, green leaves in loose clumps.

Salvia farinacea 'White porcelain.' Mealy-cup sage.

- 15 inches (38 cm).

- Plant in well-drained soil in sun.

- Multiple florets of silver-white flowers on erect stems throughout summer. Dissected silver-gray leaves.

- *S. f.* 'Victoria' has rich, violet-blue flowers.

Senecio maritima 'Silver dust.' Senecio.

- 8 inches (20 cm).

- Plant in well-drained soil in sun.

- Fernlike, silver-white foliage in low mounds.

- Grown for its foliage.

***Tropaeolum majus* var. *flore plena* 'Orange gleam.' Nasturtium.**

- 2 feet (60 cm).
- Plant in well-drained soil in sun or half-shade.
- Fragrant, deep orange to mahogany flowers all summer. Circular green leaves in open mounds.
- Quick growing, semitrailing.

***Viola tricolor* 'Baby Lucia.' Johnny-jump-up.**

- 6 inches (15 cm).
- Plant in well-drained soil in sun or half-shade.
- Small, deep lavender-blue flowers in summer. Small, semiserrated green leaves in loose clumps.
- Often self-seeds.

© Wolfgang Kaehler

Tropaeolum majus
(Nasturtium).

***Zinnia* 'Envy double.' Zinnia.**

- 2 feet (60 cm).
- Plant in well-drained soil in sun or half-shade.
- Dahlialike chartreuse-green flowers in late summer. Oval leaves in clumps.

Hardiness Zone Map

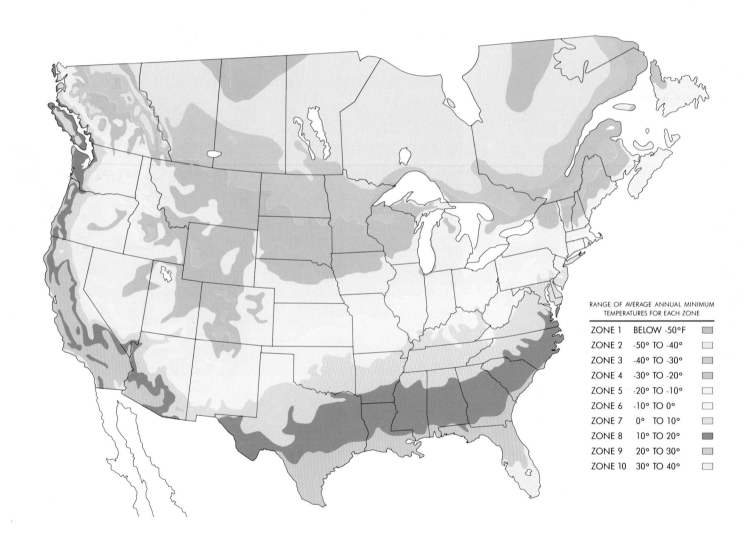

RANGE OF AVERAGE ANNUAL MINIMUM
TEMPERATURES FOR EACH ZONE

ZONE 1	BELOW -50°F	
ZONE 2	-50° TO -40°	
ZONE 3	-40° TO -30°	
ZONE 4	-30° TO -20°	
ZONE 5	-20° TO -10°	
ZONE 6	-10° TO 0°	
ZONE 7	0° TO 10°	
ZONE 8	10° TO 20°	
ZONE 9	20° TO 30°	
ZONE 10	30° TO 40°	

Sources

Armstrong Roses
P.O. Box 1020
Somis, CA 93066

California Redwood Association
591 Redwood Highway
Mill Valley, CA 94941

D.S. George Nursery
2491 Penfield Road
Fairport, NY 14450
• *Clematis*

The Garden Spot
4032 Rosewood Drive
Columbia, SC
• *Ivies*

Grate Works
Lucia Demetrios
69 Bluxcome Street
San Francisco, CA 94107
• *Sculptural, Matisse-like cut out steel grates and furniture*

Jackson & Perkins Co.
1 Rose Ln.
Wilsonville, OR 97070

Jamieson Valley Gardens
Jamieson Road, Rt. 3
Spokane, WA 99203
• *Rock garden plants*

Mini-Roses
P.O. Box 4255, Station A
Dallas, TX 75208

Moore Miniature Roses
2519 Visalia Ave.
Visalia, CA 93277

Moultrie Manufacturing Company
P.O. Drawer 1179, Dept. G11
Moultrie, GA 31776-1179

Nor'East Miniature Roses
58 Hammond St.
Rowley, MA 01969

Perry's Plants
19362 Walnut Dr.
La Puente, PA 91745
• *Ground covers*

Roses of Yesterday & Today
802-6 Brown's Valley Rd.
Watsonville, CA 95076

Siskiyou Rare Plant Nursery
2825 Cummings Road
Medford, OR 97501
• *Rock garden/plants*

Steptoe & Wife Antiques Ltd.
322 Geary Avenue
Toronto, Ontario, Canada M6H 2C7
• *Victorian design cast-iron stairs, handrails*

Tillotson's Roses
992 Brown's Valley Rd.
Watsonville, CA 95076

Bibliography

Brooks, John. *Gardens of Paradise, the History and Design of the Great Islamic Gardens.* New Amsterdam, NY: New Amsterdam Books, The Meredith Press, 1956.

Church, Thomas. *Your Private World.* San Francisco: Chronicle Books, 1969.

Gardens are for People. New York: McGraw-Hill Book Co., 1983.

Douglas, William Lake, Susan R. Frey, Norman K. Johnson, Susan Littlefield, and Michael Van Valkenburgh. *Garden Design.* New York: Simon & Schuster, 1984.

Fell, Derek. *Garden Accents.* New York: Simon & Schuster, 1987.

Fell, Derek, and Elizabeth Murray. *Home Landscaping.* New York: Simon & Schuster, 1988.

Fell, Derek, Dr. Darrell Apps, Dr. Fred Galle, Elizabeth Murray, Joan Person, and Susan Roth. *The Complete Garden Planning Manual.* Los Angeles: HP Books, 1989.

Howland, Joseph. *The House Beautiful Book of Gardens and Outdoor Living.* New York: Doubleday and Co. Inc., 1958.

Karson, Robin, and Fletcher Steele. *Landscape Architect.* New York: Harry N. Abrams, Inc./Sagapress, Inc., 1989.

Newton, Norman T. *Design of the Land: The Development of Landscape Architecture.* Cambridge: The Belknap Press of Harvard University Press, 1974.

Ortloff, Stuart H. Raymore and Henry B. Ortloff. *Garden Planning and Building.* Garden City, NY: The American Garden Guild, Inc., and Doubleday, Doran & Co., Inc., 1945.

Polyzoides, Stefanos, Roger Sherwood, and James Tice. *Courtyard Housing in Los Angeles.* Berkeley and Los Angeles: University of California Press, 1982.

Rose, Graham. *The Romantic Garden.* New York: Viking Penguin, Inc., 1988.

Sunset New Western Garden Book. Menlo Park, CA: Lane Publishing Company, 1979.

Index